Michael Andrew Law
Visit my website at www.michaelandrewlaw.com

First Printing: 2015
Shop Cheuk Yui

Introductions

These paintings are the ones of the first or/and the earliest works in the michael Andrew Law's pale hair girls series ,these paintings set the tone of the whole series that comes later on ,Law chosen half innocent ,half erotic young female figures interacted with western pop cultural and Chinese calligraphy which symbolizes the contrasting style that glued deeply in his generation , which later spawned into a 900 plus more digital-classical crossover paintings , most of the earliest in this series are done solely in oil and sometimes with acrylic based underpainting ,while later works uses more variety of materials such as glitter , gold leafs, die cuts ,sometimes museum quality achieve prints to interact with the oil and acrylic paint.

At the time when Law started working on these paintings ,he was just fresh out of his art school practice of classical oil painting in the mid 2000s in Hong Kong that's when he still using some of the academic classical painting method which he extensively trained during his art school years.that explains why These earliest work in the pale hair girls series were and mostly uses live model sitters in studio , which later on as the series expands,the later works are mostly painted based on photographs.

Law also took some of the portraits painted works from his school years, and turned them into the same visual interpretation and style with the series , a gestures,in his words ,to erases the identities of the portraits , and in attempt to creating a timelessness vibe which cooperate with the pale hair girl's identitylessness of this series.

While Michael Andrew Law obsessed with classical aesthetic figures , he also tries to pay homage to modern art superstars such as Warhol , litchenstein, richter , de Kooning, utilizing a more contemporary visual styles of images to document and expressed the contemporary predicament of his own generation - the post handover of the 2000s of Hong Kong - also cited as the most polarizing era of Hong Kong in many different subjects such as differences of political views, differences in contemporary economics situation between generations , cultural disagreement between generations and cultural differences between countries, resulting feeling and realistically of unfairness , arguments ,disappointments and finger pointing in between all of above and more.

Images in this book are also available as posters , limited edition prints ,if you interested in purchasing works or limited edition published in this book , please simply send email to info@michaelandrewlaw.com , and simply tell us this Volume's Book´s Title , Plate number or Title of the work itself , we will inform you regarding the picture 's availability as soon as possible.Other merchandise such as T-shirts , DVDs, stickers , calendar and other michael Andrew Law collectable items, please go to michaelandrewlaw.com or Google keywords "Michael Andrew Law" for further information.

PLATE No.

PLATE No.

PLATE No.

PLATE No.

PLATE No.

PLATE No.

PLATE No.

PLATE No.

PLATE No.

PLATE No.

PLATE No.

PLATE No.

PLATE No.

PLATE No.

PLATE No.

PLATE No.

PLATE No.

PLATE No.

Michael Andrew Law at Work.

Michael Andrew Law fusing digital and classical painting with west and East creative philosophy , to produce an extremely original artistic language and content that bridged west and east ,classical and modern medium , at the same time clearly tells the stories of his own generation. Combining digital creative materials and classical painting techniques with effusive yet knowing and precise focused , his paintings maintain a powerful tension between opposing aesthetic forces—expression and knowledge, control and spontaneity, savagery and wit, urbanity and primitivism—while providing satiric commentary on the oppressive realities of the predicament of Generation Internet, homegrown hongkonger's local-culture vesus Traditional Chinese culture, and The Hong Kong's post-handover history.

In his dynamically designed compositions, gracefully detailed figures and innocent faces are incise against fields that juxtaposed with portraits, chinese calligraphy, and sometimes cgi. The Pale Hair Girls Series (2006 - 2013) depicts realistic cold, icy-like young female figures surrounded by abstract and expressively painted forms and shapes revealing images of Pop culture, Historial figures, and Hong Kong landmarks.

Michael Andrew Law draws inspiration from Old Master's works such as Caravaggio , Ruben , Rembrandt , all the way to the Modern Art Superstars such as Warhol , Lichtenstein , Richter , De Kooning , Bacon , Wool and Prince . The Pale Hair Girls series mainly inspired by the painting works of French academic painter and traditionalist William-Adolphe Bouguereau and the Late Great YiFei Chen's characteristic "Romantic Realism" paintings.

In a reversal of standard East-West aesthetics, Law re-interprets Old Master's sophisticated imagery combine classical and digital materials—which resonate with Digital Vector Designs and Paintings—with fine strokes of oil paint multi-layered with paint film.In his interpretation of Leonardo Da Vinci's iconic Mona Lisa's smile (1517)—an iconic image that has been endlessly disseminated and reproduced—Law painted over the symbolism of the portrait Mona Lisa with his young wife , intent on rendering the figure in contemporary fashion with the iconic image as background .

"The Humanity triptych" depicts New Generation HongKongers in a Ruined Hong Kong city , awaiting their unknown fate of a new beginning. This painting series explores one of the central paradox of his art—between romance and derision , his romantic magnanimity as an artist and his pessimistic perspective on the predicament of Generation Y Hongkongers. Here, this paradox is symbolized by the stark contrast of icy cold young female and disturbing representations of the armageddon-like of images. Whether portrayed as single "chinese calligraphy " or in triptych composition and classical paintwork that combine both expressive and traditional painting techniques with the digital vector , the beauties and the human figures stand as eternal motifs in the history of art and also in popular culture. Both oppositional and parallel, they are reminders of the fragile vibrancy of life and the impitoyable passing of time.

A references between different cultural refrence (high/pop, classical/contemporary, east/west), Michael Andrew Law has stated that an artist should be someone who understood how to hybrid between different worlds and go ahead makes an effort to knowing them. With his distinctive "iEgoism" philosophy , which employs highly refined academic painting techniques to depict a mixture of abstract expressionism within a representational pop culture images. These techniques parallel to the themes of romance and predicament of this generation , he recollects and revitalizes narratives of irony and introspection.

Michael Andrew Law was born in 1982 in British Hong Kong , studied fine art with american artist Daniel Anderson and with artist graduatee of China Central Academy of Fine Arts Sam Zeng from 2003 - 2006 . He co-founded the Hong Kong Art Studio Nature Art Workshop in 2008. In addition to the production and marketing of Michael Andrew Law's art and related work, Nature Art functions as a supportive environment for the
fostering of emerging Hong Konger artists. Law is also a curator. In 2013, he organized an exhibition of contemporary art titled "iEgoism ," which served as a commentaries of contemporary HongKong Gen Y pop culture ;These Theroy also published in the book : "iEgoism" in 2014.

Michael Andrew Law currently works and lives in Hong Kong.

For further information please contact the studio at info@michaelandrewlaw.com or at +852.6444.7550. All images are subject to copyright. Artist/Studio/Gallery's approval must be granted prior to reproduction.

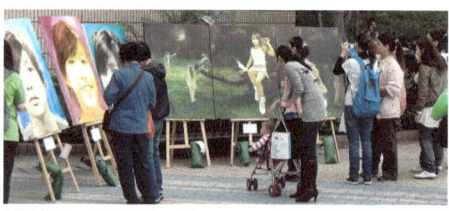

2010 Avenue of Stars, Hong Kong

Exhibition :

2013 DeTour Matters 2013 Satellite Events at NatureArt Gallery
2013 December to Remember , One man show at NatureArt Gallery Central District, Hong Kong.
2012 Solo Show , Park Central tseung kwan O ,Hong Kong
2011 Art Walk Group Showing , Discovery Bay ,Hong Kong
2011 HK Gold Coast (Book signing exhibition)
2009 Solo Painting Exhibition The Avenue of Stars
Group Exhibition of Daniel Anderson workshop Classical Realism class of 2008 at Manhattan,NY
2007 Guest and Exhibition The Peak Galleria Hong Kong
2007 Invited workshop exhibition, Elements, Hong Kong
Group Exhibition of Classical Realism class of 2007 at Manhattan,NY
2006 Collection by Cardinal Zen Ze-kiun and exhibited at Catholic Church of Hong Kong.
2004 - 2007, Hong Kong Young Artist Group Exhibition, Hong Kong Central Library.
Group Exhibition of Classical Realism class of 2006 at East Village, Manhattan,NY
2005 Illustration original exhibition for Kung Kao Po
2004 Group Exhibition, Wanchai Tower
2003 Group Exhibition, Hong Kong Convention and Exhibition Centre.
2003 Winner of I luv Hong Kong Painting Competition, exhibition at The Landmark (Hong Kong).
2002 The Holy story Picture Book illustrated picture original exhibition ,sai wan ho civic centre.

SELECTED COLLECTIONS :

Cardinal of the Catholic Church Joseph Zen Ze-kiun
Organic Beauty Inc
Agriculture, Fisheries and Conservation Department
Ms.Ho Wei Ying
Ms. Annie Yu
Daniel Anderson
MR.Tsang Yan Sam

PUBLICATIONS :

Fisheye magazine , featured artist interview , November 2002
Kung Kao Po , interview , June 2006
Art of Rock Realism , 2006
The Art of Michael Andrew Law , 2010
December to Remember One man Show Art Book , 2013
iEgoism , 2015

Solo Shows 2010 - 2013

Available Now!

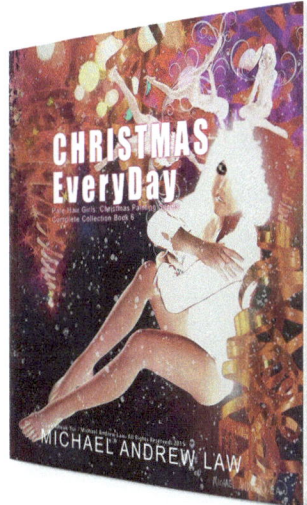

I really appreciate your purchase of this Painting

Collection Book , I hope you enjoy reading them as

much as I enjoyed painting them!

May God bless your home with peace, joy and love.

From Michael Andrew Law.

Find Me Online.

Michael Andrew Law 🔍

www.ingramcontent.com/pod-product-compliance
Lightning Source LLC
Chambersburg PA
CBHW042024200526
45159CB00036B/1812